The Word a

Classic Devotions from the Minor Prophets

THE WORD AND PRAYER

Classic Devotions from the Minor Prophets

JOHN CALVIN

Edited by Charles E. Edwards

SOLID GROUND CHRISTIAN BOOKS
Birmingham, Alabama USA

SOLID GROUND CHRISTIAN BOOKS
PO Box 660132, Vestavia Hills, AL 35266
205-443-0311
sgcb@charter.net
http://www.solid-ground-books.com

The Word and Prayer:
Classic Devotions from the Minor Prophets

by John Calvin (1509-1564)
edited by Charles E. Edwards

From the 1897 edition by Presbyterian Board of Publication,
And Sabbath School Work, Philadelphia, PA

Published by Solid Ground Christian Books

Classic Reprints Series

First printing January 2005

ISBN: 1-932474-69-2

Cover design by Borgo Design, Tuscaloosa, Alabama.
Contact them at nelbrown@comcast.net

Manufactured in the United States of America

TABLE OF CONTENTS

Introduction

JOHN CALVIN was a man of God. He has been justly admired as the theologian of the Reformation; as the prince of commentators upon Holy Scripture, and the father of its scientific exegesis, and as the virtual founder of American common schools. He was also great in prayer. The system of Christian doctrine which bears his name has ever been the mother of devotion. It may be known by its fruits; for it has trained a noble army of martyrs, reformers, missionaries, and evangelists. It has inspired countless revivals of religion.[1] It lives in all the popular hymnals of Christendom. Prayer is the "vital breath," the "native air" of Calvinism. The prayers of John Calvin, however, have received little attention, as compared with the fame which crowns his theological writings. His commentaries upon Jeremiah, Ezekiel, Daniel, and the Minor Prophets were originally delivered in the form of lectures, each followed by appropriate petitions. Both lectures and prayers were extemporaneous. In his epistle dedicatory, prefaced to the commentary upon the Minor Prophets, and addressed to the King of Sweden, Calvin says: "Had it been in my power I would rather have tried to prevent the wider circulation of

---

[1] For clear evidence of these statements see *Calvinism in History* by Nathaniel S. McFetridge, recently republished by Solid Ground Christian Books (Nov. 2004).

that extemporaneous kind of teaching, intended for the particular benefit of my auditory, and with which benefit I was abundantly satisfied." John Budaeus,[2] in another preface, piously exhorts that we pray for the Spirit of God, that we may come to the reading of Scripture instructed by him. "And for this end," he says, "much help may be given us by the short prayers which we have taken care to add at the close of every lecture as gathered by us with the same care and fidelity as the lectures were; and the ignorant may also have in these a pattern, as it were, painted before them, by which they may form their prayers from the words of Scripture. For as at the beginning of the lectures he ever used the same form of prayer, so he was wont ever to finish every lecture by a new prayer formed at the time, as given him by the Spirit of God, and accommodated to the subject of the lecture."

The following passage from Calvin's commentary on Genesis shows how his oratory rises sometimes to the sublime: "It is vain for any to reason as philosophers on the workmanship of the world, except those who having been first humbled by the preaching of the gospel have learned to submit the whole of their intellectual wisdom (as Paul expresses it) to the foolishness of the cross. Nothing shall we find, I say, above or below, which can raise us up to God, until Christ shall have instructed us in his own school. Yet this cannot be done unless we, having emerged out of the lowest depths, are borne up above all heavens in the chariot of his cross, that there by faith we may apprehend those things which the eye has never seen, the ear never heard, and which far surpass our hearts and minds. There the invisible

---

[2] One of the men who labored in Geneva with Calvin to help edit his notes on the Prophets for publication.

kingdom of Christ fills all things, and his spiritual grace is diffused through all. Yet this does not prevent us from applying our senses to the consideration of heaven and earth, that we may thence seek confirmation in the true knowledge of God. For Christ is that image in which God presents to our view not only his heart, but also his hands and his feet. I give the name of his *heart* to that secret love with which he embraces us in Christ, by his *hands* and *feet* I understand those works of his which are displayed before our eyes." His translator notes here that Calvin shows an intimate experimental acquaintance with the declaration of the apostle, "And made us sit together in heavenly places in Christ Jesus."[3]

Calvin's correspondence indicates how earnestly he watched and prayed for the salvation of our English and Scottish forefathers.

To his ardent disciple John Knox he writes: "It was a source of pleasure, not to me only, but to all the pious persons to whom I communicated the agreeable tidings, to hear of the very real success which has crowned your labors. But as we are astonished at such incredible progress in so brief a space of time, so we likewise give thanks to God whose extraordinary blessing is signally displayed herein."

In his suggestions to the Protector Somerset, he remarks: "Monsignor, it appears to me that there is very little preaching of a lively kind in the kingdom, but that the greater part deliver it by way of reading from a written discourse. Now this preaching ought not to be lifeless, but lively, to teach, to exhort, to reprove, as St. Paul says in speaking to Timothy (II Tim. 4:2).

---

[3] Ephesians 2:6.

So indeed, that if an unbeliever enter, he may be so effectually arrested and convinced as to give glory to God, as Paul says in another passage (I Cor. 14). You are also aware, Monsignor, how he speaks of the lively power and energy with which they ought to speak, who would approve themselves as good and faithful ministers of God, who must not make a parade of rhetoric, only to gain esteem for themselves, but that the Spirit of God ought to sound forth by their voice, so as to work with mighty energy."

His letter to the boy-king, Edward the Sixth, deserves undying remembrance: "It is indeed a great thing to be a king, and yet more over such a country, nevertheless, I have no doubt that you reckon it beyond comparison better to be a Christian. It is therefore an invaluable privilege that God has vouchsafed you, sire, to be a Christian king, to serve as his lieutenant in ordering and maintaining the kingdom of Jesus Christ in England."

Lady Anne Seymour, daughter of the Protector Somerset, receives this message from him "Certainly among so many gifts with which God has endowed and adorned you, this stands unquestionably first—that he stretched out his hand to you in tender childhood to lead you to his own Son, who is the author of eternal salvation, and the fountain of all good."

Cranmer was one of his correspondents and co-laborers. He submitted to Calvin a proposal for a General Synod for the more close union of the Reformed churches. Calvin thus communicates his approval: "So much does this concern me that could I be of any service I would not grudge to cross even ten seas if need were on account of it." In another letter he says: "I highly commend the plan which your reverend sir, have adopted to make the English frame for themselves, without delay, a religious constitution, lest by matters remaining longer in an unsettled state, or not being sufficiently digested, the minds of the common people should be confirmed in suspense."

He wrote to Farel: "The Archbishop of Canterbury informed me that I could do nothing more useful than to write to the King more frequently. This gave me more pleasure than if I had come to the possession of a great sum of money."

When English exiles were scattered over the continent by Queen Mary's persecution Calvin's pen was exercised in their behalf. He welcomed them to the hospitality of Geneva, and thus revealed his sympathy: "We have good reason to feel anxiety—yea even torment—regarding that nation [England]. Scarcely has any other thing so distressed me as this English affair."

Upon the accession of Queen Elizabeth, Calvin dedicated to her a new edition of his commentary on Isaiah, in which he grandly pleads for the gospel: "It is not so much my object to be favored with your countenance in my personal labors as humbly to entreat, and by the sacred name of Christ to implore, not only that through your kindness all orthodox books may again be welcomed and freely circulated in England, but that your chief care may be directed to promote religion, which has fallen into shameful neglect. And if this is justly demanded from all kings of the earth by the only begotten Son of God, by a still more sacred tie does he hold you bound, most noble Queen, to perform this duty, for when even you, though a King's daughter, were not exempted from that dreadful storm which fell with severity on the heads of all the godly, by the wonderful manner in which he brought you out safe, though not unmoved by the fear of danger, he has laid you under obligation to devote yourself and all your exertions to his service. So far are you from having any reason to be ashamed of this deliverance that God has given you large and abundant grounds of boasting by conforming you to the image of his Son, on whom the prophet Isaiah bestows this among other commendations, that from prison and from judgment he was raised to the loftiest height of heavenly dominion."

The desire of this great reformer is thus expressed to Bucer: "I pray that the English may make a stand for the genuine purity of Christianity, until everything in that country is seen to be regulated according to the rule which Christ himself has laid down."

The prayer of Calvin has been wonderfully answered. England was the bulwark of the Reformation. By the defeat of the Spanish Armada she became mistress of the seas. The sea power of the world then passed from Catholic to Protestant hands, which have firmly held it ever since. The English Puritan movement was Calvinistic to the core. As a result, the Westminster standards, the most complete of Calvinistic creeds, were formulated by the "first among Protestant councils,"[4] and adopted by the British Parliament. Green says: "The whole history of English progress since the Restoration, on its moral and spiritual sides, has been the history of Puritanism."[5] The majority of Calvinists now speak the English language. Dr. Schaff says:[6] "His religious influence upon the Anglo-Saxon race in both continents is greater than that of any native

---

[4] Schaff, *Creeds of Christendom*, Vol. I, p. 728.
[5] *Short History of the English People*, Vol. III, chap. VIII *ad fin.*
[6] *History of the Christian Church*, Vol. VII, pp. 806,7.

Englishman, and continues to this day." He quotes Baroness Bunsen's eulogy: "The merit of Calvin is his own, and he has been the creative instrument of the strength of England, of Scotland, of the United States of America."

The Calvin Translation Society has enriched English literature by the publication of a large part of his works in fifty-two noble volumes. Their translation has been revised for this brief compilation, which has been drawn entirely from the commentaries on the Minor Prophets. The hundreds of lectures and prayers found in his other writings are equally edifying, and deserve a world-wide circulation.

In conclusion, an exhortation taken from a quaint English translation of Calvin's homilies on Deuteronomy, and similar to many others which occur at the end of his sermons, is appropriate for the devout reader of the sentence prayers which follow: "Now let us kneel down in the presence of our good God, with acknowledgement of our faults, praying him to make us feel them more and more, that we may run wholly unto him, and that forasmuch as we have not now a Moses to lead us into the land of Canaan, but Jesus Christ, which is come down unto us to draw us up into heaven after him, we may follow such a guide, yielding ourselves wholly unto him, and in no wise dragging back from him, that it may please him to grant this grace, not only to us, but also to all people and nations of the earth."

Charles E. Edwards

The prayer which Calvin was accustomed to use at the beginning of his lectures:

"May the Lord grant that we may engage in contemplating the mysteries of his heavenly wisdom with really increasing devotion, to his glory and to our edification. Amen."

1

The Solitary Lamb

For Israel slideth back as a backsliding heifer: now the LORD will feed them as a lamb in a large place.—Hosea 4:16

It is what is peculiar to sheep, we know, that they continue under the shepherd's care: and a sheep, when driven into solitude, shows itself by its bleating to be timid, and to be as it were seeking its shepherd and its flock. In short, a sheep is not a solitary animal; and it is to sheep and lambs almost a part of their food to feed together, and also under the eye of him under whose care they are. Now there seems to be here a most striking change of figure: They are, says the prophet, like untamable heifers, for they are so wanton that no field can satisfy their wantonness, as when a heifer would occupy the whole land. "Such then," he says, "and so outrageous is the disobedience of this people that they can no longer endure, except a spacious place be given to each of them. I will therefore give them a spacious place: but for this end, that each of them may be like a lamb, which looks around and sees no flock to which it may join itself."

Prayer

Grant, Almighty God, that since thou hast deigned in thy mercy to gather us to thy Church, and to enclose us within the boundaries of thy word, by which thou preserveth us in the true and right worship of thy majesty, O grant that we may continue contented in this obedience to thee; and though Satan may, in many ways, attempt to draw us here and there, and we be also ourselves by nature inclined to evil, O grant, that being confirmed in faith and united to thee by that sacred bond, we may yet constantly abide under the restraint of thy word, and thus cleave to Christ thine only begotten Son who has joined us forever to himself, and that we may never by any means turn aside from thee, but be, on the contrary, confirmed in the faith of his gospel, until at length he will receive us all into his kingdom. Amen.

2

A Sovereign Word

Hear ye this, O priests; and hearken, ye house of Israel; and give ye ear, O house of the king; for judgment is toward you, because ye have been a snare on Mizpah, and a net spread upon Tabor.
—Hosea 5:1

The prophet here preaches against the whole people; but he mainly directs his discourse to the priests and the rulers; for they were the source of the prevailing evils: the priests, intent on gain, neglected the worship of God; and the chief men were become in every way corrupt. . . . Even kings are not exempted from the duty of learning what is commonly taught, if they wish to be counted members of the Church; for the Lord would have all, without exception, to be ruled by his word; and he takes this as a proof of men's obedience, their submission to his word. And as kings think themselves separated from the general class of men, the prophet here shows that he was sent to the king and his counselors. The same reason holds good as to priests, for as the dignity of their order is the highest, so this impiety has prevailed in all ages that the priests think themselves at liberty to do what they please. Let us know that in the Church the word of God so possesses the highest rank that neither priests, nor kings, nor their counselors can claim a privilege to themselves, as though their conduct was not to be subject to God's word.

Prayer

Grant, Almighty God, that since thou continuest daily to exhort us, and though thou seest us often turning aside from the right course, thou yet ceasest not to stretch forth thy hand to us, and also to rouse us by reproofs that we may repent,—O grant that we may not be permitted to reject thy word with such perverseness as thou condemnest here in thine ancient people by the mouth of thy prophet; but rule us by thy Spirit, that we may meekly and obediently submit to thee, and with such teachableness, that if we have not hitherto been willing to become wise, we may not at least be incurable, but suffer thee to heal our diseases, so that we may truly repent, and be so wholly given to obey thee, as never to attempt anything beyond the rule of thy word, and without that wisdom which thou hast revealed to us, not only by Moses and thy prophets, but also by thine only begotten Son our Lord Jesus Christ. Amen.

3

Kindness and Faith

For I desired mercy, and not sacrifice; and the knowledge of God more than burnt offerings.—Hosea 6:6

This is a remarkable passage; the Son of God has twice quoted it. The Pharisees reproached him for his intercourse with men of bad and abandoned life, and he said to them in the ninth chapter of Matthew, "Mercy I desire and not sacrifice." He shows by this defense, that God is not worshiped by external ceremonies, but when men forgive and bear with one another and are not above measure rigid. Again, when the Pharisees blamed the disciples for gathering ears of corn, Christ shows that those who make holiness to consist in ceremonies are foolish worshipers of God; and that they also blamed their brethren without a cause, and made a crime of what was not in itself sinful, and what could be easily defended by any wise and calm expounder. These two clauses ought to be read conjointly—that kindness pleases God—and that faith pleases God. Faith by itself cannot please God, since it cannot even exist without love to our neighbor; and then, human kindness is not sufficient; for were any one to abstain from doing any injury, and from hurting his brethren in any thing, he might still be a profane man, and a despiser of God; and certainly his kindness would be then of no avail to him. It is also worthy of being observed, that he calls faith the knowledge of God.

Prayer

Grant, Almighty God, that as we are prone to every kind of wickedness and are easily led away to imitate it, when there is any excuse for going astray and any opportunity is offered,—O grant, that being strengthened by the help of thy Spirit, we may continue in purity of faith, and that what we have learnt concerning thee, that thou art a Spirit, may so profit us, that we may worship the in spirit, and with a sincere heart, and never turn aside after the corruptions of the world, nor think that we can deceive thee; but may we so devote our souls and our bodies to thee, that our life may in every part of it testify, that we are a pure and holy sacrifice to thee in Christ Jesus our Lord. Amen.

4

Sin and Punishment

They have deeply corrupted *themselves*, as in the days of Gibeah: *therefore* he will remember their iniquity, he will visit their sins.
—Hosea 9:9.

Hosea declares here, that the people were so sunk in their vices that they could not be drawn out of them. He who has fallen can raise himself up when one extends a hand to him; and he who strives to emerge from the mire, finding a helper to assist him, can plant his foot again on solid ground; but when he is cast into a gulf he has no hope of a recovery. I extend my hand in vain when one sinks in a shipwreck and is fallen into a vast whirlpool. Let us hence also learn to rouse ourselves; and let us, in the first place, notice what the prophet says of the Israelites, that they were deeply engulfed; for men must be filled with contempt to God when they thus descend into the deep. Let, then, each of us stir up himself daily to repentance, and carefully beware lest he should descend into this vast whirlpool. Let us know that they are greatly deceived who indulge themselves as long as the Lord mercifully bears with their sins; for though he may for a time conceal his displeasure, at a time he will remember, and prove that he does so by executing a just punishment.

Prayer

Grant, Almighty God, that as thou shinest on us by thy word, we may not be blind at midday, nor willfully seek darkness, and thus lull our minds asleep: but may we be roused daily by thy words, and may we stir up ourselves more and more to fear thy name and thus present ourselves and all our pursuits, as a sacrifice to thee, that thou mayest peaceably rule, and perpetually dwell in us, until thou gatherest us to thy celestial habitation, where there is reserved for us eternal rest and glory through Jesus Christ our Lord. Amen.

5

The Divinity of Christ

*Yea, he had power over the angel, and prevailed: he wept, and made
supplication unto him: he found him in Bethel, and there he spake
with us; Even the LORD God of hosts; the LORD is his memorial.
—Hosea 12:4,5.*

It must be noticed that the prophet here testifies that
he was the eternal and the only true God, who yet was
at the same time an angel. But it may be asked, How
was he the eternal God and at the same time an
angel? When the Lord appeared by his angels, the
name of Jehovah was given to them; not, indeed, to all
the angels indiscriminately, but to the chief angel, by
whom God manifested himself. It then follows that this
angel was truly and essentially God. But this would not
strictly apply to God, except there be some distinction
of persons. There must then be some person in the
Deity to whom this name and title of an angel can
apply; for if we take the name, God, without difference
or distinction, and regard it as denoting his essence, it
would certainly be inconsistent to say that he is God
and an angel too; but when we distinguish persons in
the Deity, there is no inconsistency. How so? Because
Christ, the eternal Wisdom of God, did put on the
character of a Mediator before he put on our flesh. He
was therefore, then, a Mediator, and in that capacity
he was also an angel. He was at the same time
Jehovah, who is now God manifested in the flesh.

18

Prayer

Grant, Almighty God, that inasmuch as thou showest thyself to us at this day so kindly as a Father, having presented to us a singular and an invaluable pledge of thy favor in thine only begotten Son,—O grant that we may entirely devote ourselves to thee, and truly render thee that free service and obedience which is due to a Father, so that we may have no other object throughout life but to confirm that adoption with which thou hast favored us once for all, until at length we shall partake of its fruit when thou dost gather us into thine eternal kingdom, together with Jesus Christ thine only Son. Amen.

6

A Gracious Reminder

I did know thee in the wilderness, in the land of great drought.
—Hosea 13:5.

He says, "I have manifested myself to thee from the land of Egypt, from thy very nativity. Thou didst then begin to live, and to be some sort of people, when I stretched forth my hand to thee." The people were redeemed on this condition that they should devote themselves wholly to God. As we are at this day Christ's, and no one of us ought to live according to his own will, for Christ died and rose again for this end, that he might be the Lord of the living and of the dead: so also then, the Israelites had been redeemed by God that they might offer themselves wholly to him. If this one God was sufficient for redeeming his people, what do the people now mean, when they wander and seek aid here and there? For they ought to render to God the life received from him, which they now enjoy, and ought to acknowledge it to be sufficiently safe under his sole protection. We learn that the worship of God does not consist in words, but in faith and hope and prayer.

Prayer

Grant, Almighty God, that as thou dost so kindly urge us daily by thy voice, meekly and calmly to offer ourselves to be ruled by thee, and since thou hast exalted us to the highest degree of honor by freeing us from the dread of the devil, and from that tyranny which kept us in miserable fear, and hast also favored us with the spirit of adoption and of assurance,—O grant that we, being mindful of these benefits, may ever submit ourselves to thee, and desire only to raise our voice for this end, that the whole world may submit itself to thee, and that those who seem now to rage against thee may at length be brought, as well as we, to render thee obedience so that thy Son Christ may be the Lord of all to the end that thou alone mayest be exalted, and that we may be made subject to thee and be at length raised up above and become partakers of that glory which has been obtained for us by Christ alone, our Lord. Amen.

7

The True King

I will be thy king: where *is any other* that may save thee in all thy
cities? and thy judges of whom thou saidst, 'Give me a king and
princes?' —Hosea 13:10.

God repeats what he had before declared, that he
would always be the same: "Though the Israelites rail
against me, that I do not pursue my usual course of
kindness, it is yet most false; for I remain ever the
same, and am always ready to show kindness to men;
for I do not, as I have elsewhere declared, forsake the
work of my hands (Psalm 138:8). Seeing then that I
thus continue my favor toward men, it must be that
the way to my favor is closed up by their wickedness.
Let them therefore examine themselves, when they
cry and I answer not. When in their evils they in a
manner pine away, and find no relief, let them
acknowledge it to be their own fault; for I would have
made myself the same as ever I have been, and they
would have found me a deliverer, had not a change
taken place in them."

Prayer

Grant, Almighty God, that as thou hast given us once for all thine only begotten Son to rule us, and hast by thy good pleasure consecrated him a King over us, that we may be perpetually safe and secure under his hand against all the attempts of the devil and of the whole world,—O grant, that we may suffer ourselves to be ruled by his authority, and so conduct ourselves, that he himself may ever continue to watch for our safety: and as thou hast committed us to him, that he may be the guardian of our salvation, so also suffer us neither to turn aside nor fall, but preserve us ever in his service, until we at length be gathered into that blessed and everlasting kingdom, which has been procured for us by the blood of thine only Son. Amen.

8

A Kind Invitation

O Israel, return unto the LORD thy God; for thou hast fallen by thine iniquity.—Hosea 14:1.

Here the prophet exhorts the Israelites to repentance, and still propounds some hope of mercy. But this may seem inconsistent, as he had already testified that there would be no remedy any more, because they had extremely provoked God. But the solution is ready at hand, and it is this: In speaking before of the final destruction of the people, he had respect to the whole body of the people; but now he directs his discourse to the few who had as yet remained faithful. And this distinction ought to be carefully noticed; otherwise we shall find ourselves perplexed in many parts of Scripture. God had now, indeed, determined to destroy them, and he wished this to be made known to them by the preaching of Hosea. But yet God had ever some seed remaining among his chosen people; some sound members remained, as in a large heap of chaff some grains may be found concealed. His discourse here ought to be especially applied to the elect of God, who, although they had fallen away for a time, and had become entangled in the common vices of the age, were yet not altogether incurable. The prophet now kindly invites them, for he could not succeed by severe words without mingling a hope of favor, as we know that there can be no hope of repentance without faith.

Prayer

Grant, Almighty God, that as we now carry about us this mortal body, yea, and nourish through sin a thousand deaths within us,—O grant that we may ever by faith direct our eyes toward heaven, and to that incomprehensible power, which is to be manifested at the last day by Jesus Christ our Lord, so that in the midst of death we may hope that thou wilt be our Redeemer, and enjoy that redemption which he completed when he rose from the dead, and not doubt that the fruit which he then brought forth by his Spirit will come also to us when Christ himself shall come to judge the world; and may we thus walk in the fear of thy name, that we may be really gathered among his members, to be made partakers of that glory which by his death he has procured for us. Amen

9

Worship and Joy

Is not the meat cut off before our eyes, *yea*, joy and gladness from the house of our God?—Joel 1:16.

The prophet here chides the madness of the Jews that they perceived not things set before their eyes. He therefore says that they were blind in the midst of light, and that their sight was such that seeing they saw nothing; they surely ought to have felt distressed, when want reached even to the temple. For since God had commanded the first-fruits to be offered to him, certainly the temple ought to have been honored with its sacrifices; and though mortals perish a hundred times through famine and want, yet God ought not to be defrauded of his right. He afterwards adds that joy and gladness were taken away; for God commanded the Jews to come to the temple to give thanks and to acknowledge themselves blessed, because he had chosen his habitation among them. Hence this expression is so often repeated by Moses, "Thou shalt rejoice before thy God;" for by saying this God intended to encourage the people the more to come cheerfully to the temple; as though he said, "I certainly need not your presence, but I wish by my presence to make you glad." But now when the worship of God ceased, the prophet says that joy had also been abolished; for the Jews could not cheerfully give thanks to God when his curse was before their eyes.

Prayer

Grant, Almighty God, that as thou seest us to be surrounded with the infirmity of our flesh, and so held by, and as it were, overwhelmed with earthly cares, that we can hardly raise up our hearts and minds to thee,—O grant that being awaked by thy word and daily warnings we may at length feel our evils, and that we may not only learn by the stripes thou inflictest on us, but also of our own accord, summon ourselves to judgment, and examine our hearts and thus come to thy presence, being our own judges; so that we may anticipate thy displeasure and thus obtain that mercy which thou hast promised to all who, turning only to thee, deprecate thy wrath and also hope for thy favor through the name of our Lord Jesus Christ. Amen.

10

Sounding the Alarm

Blow ye the trumpet in Zion, and sound an alarm in my holy mountain: let all the inhabitants of the land tremble: for the day of the Loan cometh, for *it is* nigh at hand.—Joel 2:1.

This chapter contains serious exhortations, mixed with threatenings, but the prophet threatens for the purpose of correcting the indifference of the people, who were very slow to consider God's judgments. The object of the narrative, then, is to make the people sensible that it was now no time for taking rest.

The prophet begins with an exhortation. We know, indeed, that he alludes to the usual customs sanctioned by the law, for, as on festivals trumpets were sounded to call the people, so also it was done when anything extraordinary happened. Hence, the prophet addresses not each individually, but, as all had done wickedly, from the least to the greatest, he bids the whole assembly to be called, that they may in common own themselves to be guilty before God, and deprecate his vengeance. This passage shows that when any judgment of God is impending, and tokens of it appear, this remedy ought to be used, namely, that all must publicly assemble and confess themselves worthy of punishment, and at the same time flee to the mercy of God. This, we know, was formerly enjoined upon the people, and this practice has not been abolished by the gospel.

Prayer

Grant, Almighty God, that as thou invitest us daily with so much kindness and love, and makest known to us thy paternal good-will which thou didst once for all show to us in Christ thy Son,—O grant that, being allured by thy goodness, we may surrender ourselves to thee and become so teachable and submissive that wherever thou guidest us by thy Spirit thou mayest follow us with every blessing. Let us not, in the meantime, be deaf to thy warnings; and whenever we deviate from the right way, grant that we may immediately awake when thou warnest us, and return to the right path, and deign thou also to embrace us and reconcile us to thyself through Christ our only Lord. Amen.

11

The Outpouring of the Spirit

And it shall come to pass afterward, that I will pour out my spirit upon all flesh; and your sons and your daughters shall prophesy, your old men shall dream dreams, your young men shall see visions. —Joel 2:28.

The prophet after having set before them the rudiments as though they were children, now brings before them a more complete doctrine (for thus they were to be led) and affords them a taste of the favor of God in its external signs. "Ascend, then, now," he says, "to spiritual life, for the fountain is one and the same, though when earthly benefits occupy and engross your attention ye no doubt pollute them. But God feeds you, not to fill and pamper you, for he would not have you to be like brute animals. Then know that your bodies are fed, and that God gives support to you, that ye may aspire after spiritual life, for he leads you to this as by the hand; be this, then, your object." He began with temporal benefits, for it was needful that an untutored people should be thus led by degrees, that on account of their infirmity, sluggishness, and dullness, they might thus make better progress until they understood that God would for this end be a Father to them.

Prayer

Grant, Almighty God, that since we want so many aids while in this frail life, and as it is a shadowy life, we cannot pass a moment except thou dost continually and at all times supply through thy bounty what is needful,—O grant, that we may so profit by thy so many benefits, that we may learn to raise our minds upward and ever aspire after celestial life to which by thy gospel thou invitest us so kindly and sweetly every day, that being gathered into thy celestial kingdom, we may enjoy that perfect felicity which has been procured for us by the blood of thy Son our Lord Jesus Christ. Amen.

12

An Admonition

And I will show wonders in the heavens and in the earth, blood, and fire, and pillars of smoke. The sun shall be turned into darkness, and the moon into blood, before the great and the terrible day of the LORD come.—Joel 2:30, 31

The prophet had hitherto promised that God would deal kindly and bountifully with his people; and everything he has said tended to elevate the spirits of the people and fill them with joy. But now he seems again to threaten them with God's wrath and to strike miserable men with fear, who had not, as yet recovered breath; for at the time the prophet spoke the Jews, we know, were in the greatest sorrow. But it is rather an admonition than a threatening. The prophet warns them of what would be lest the faithful should promise themselves an exemption from all cares and troubles: for we know how prone men are to self-indulgence. Hence the prophet reminds us that though God would bountifully feed his Church, and testify by external tokens his paternal love, and though he would pour out his Spirit (a token far more remarkable), yet the faithful would continue to be distressed with many troubles. For God designs not to deal too delicately with his Church on earth; but when he gives tokens of his kindness, he at the same time mingles some exercises for patience, lest the faithful should become self-indulgent or sleep on earthly blessings, but that they may ever seek higher things.

Prayer

Grant, Almighty God, that as we are now surrounded on every side by so many miseries, and as our condition is such that amidst groans and continual sorrows our life could be hardly sustained unless thou dost support us by spiritual grace,—O grant, that we may learn to look upon the face of thine Anointed and seek comfort from him in our misfortunes, and such a comfort as may not engross our minds, or at least retain us in the world, but raise our thoughts to heaven and daily seal to our hearts the testimony of our adoption, and that though many evils must be borne by us in this world we may yet continue to pursue our course and to fight and strive with invincible perseverance, until having at length finished all our struggles, we reach that blessed rest which has been obtained for us by the blood of thine only-begotten Son our Lord Jesus Christ. Amen.

13

Calling on the Lord

And it shall come to pass, *that* whosoever shall call on the name of the LORD shall be delivered: for in mount Zion and in Jerusalem shall be deliverance, as the LORD hath said, and in the remnant whom the LORD shall call.—Joel 2:32.

God declares that the invocation of his name in a despairing condition is a sure port of safety. What the prophet had said was certainly dreadful,—that the whole order of nature would be so changed that no spark of life would appear, and that all places would be filled with darkness. What, therefore, he says now is the same as though he declared that if men called on the name of God life would be found in the grave. Since then God invites here the lost and the dead, there is no reason why even the heaviest distresses should preclude an access for us or for our prayers. If there is promised salvation and deliverance to all who shall call on the name of the Lord, it follows, as Paul reasons, that the doctrine of the gospel belongs to the Gentiles also. It would have been a great presumption in us to present ourselves before God, except he had given us confidence and promised to hear us. We learn from this place that however much God may afflict his Church, it will yet be perpetuated in the world; for it can no more be destroyed than the very truth of God, which is eternal and immutable.

Prayer

Grant, Almighty God, that as thou not only invitest us continually by the voice of thy gospel to seek thee, but also offerest to us thy Son as our Mediator, through whom an access to thee is open, that we may find thee a propitious Father,—O grant, that relying on thy kind invitation, we may through life exercise ourselves in prayer, and as so many evils disturb us on all sides and so many wants distress and oppress us, may we be led more earnestly to call on thee, and in the meanwhile be never wearied in this exercise of prayer; until having been heard by thee throughout life, we may at length be gathered to thine eternal kingdom where we shall enjoy that salvation which thou hast promised to us, and of which also thou daily testifiest to us by thy gospel, and be forever united to thine only-begotten Son of whom we are now members; that we may be partakers of all the blessings which he has obtained for us by his death. Amen.

14

A Blessed Experience

So shall ye know that I *am* the LORD your God dwelling in Zion, my holy mountain: then shall Jerusalem be holy, and there shall no strangers pass through her any more. —Joel 3:17.

The prophet intimates that the favor of God had been so hidden during the afflictions of the people that they could but think that they were forsaken by God. His word ought indeed to be sufficient for us in the greatest evils; for though God may cast us into the deepest gulfs, yet when he shines upon us by his word it ought to be a consolation abundantly availing to sustain our souls.

There is a twofold knowledge, the knowledge of faith, received from his word, and the knowledge of experience, as we say, derived from actual enjoyment. The faithful ever acknowledge that salvation is laid up for them in God; but sometimes they do not by actual enjoyment know God to be their Father. The prophet therefore now treats of real knowledge when he says that they shall know that they have a God. How are they to know this? By experience. This passage teaches us that though God should not put forth his hand manifestly to help us, we ought yet to entertain good hope of his favor; for the prophet spoke for this end, that the godly might, before the event or the accomplishment of the prophecy should come, look to God and cast all their cares on him.

Prayer

Grant, Almighty God, that as we have, in this world, to fight continually, not only with one kind of enemies, but with innumerable ones, and not only with flesh and blood, but also with the devil, the prince of darkness,—O grant that being armed with thy power we may steadily persevere in this contest; and when thou afflictest us for our sins, may we learn to humble ourselves and so submit to thy authority that we may hope for the redemption promised to us; and though tokens of thy displeasure may often appear to us, may we yet ever raise up our minds by hope to heaven and from thence look for thine only-begotten Son, until, coming as Judge of the world, he assembles us for the enjoyment of that blessed and eternal life which he has obtained for us by his own blood. Amen.

15

The Law of Worship

'And offer a sacrifice of thanksgiving with leaven, and proclaim *and* publish the free offerings: for this liketh you, O ye children of Israel,' saith the Lord God.—Amos 4:5.

By saying that the Israelites loved to do these things, he upbraids their presumption in devising at their own will new modes of worship, as though he said, "I require no sacrifices from you except those offered at Jerusalem, but ye offer them to me in a profane place. Therefore regard your sacrifices as offered to yourselves, and not to me." We, indeed, know how hypocrites ever make God a debtor to themselves; when they undertake any labor in their frivolous ceremonies, they think that God is bound to them. "Ye ought to have consulted me and simply to have obeyed my word, to have regarded what pleased me, what I have commanded; but ye have despised my word, neglected my law, and followed what pleased yourselves and proceeded from your own fancies. Since, then, your own will is your law, seek a recompense from yourselves, for I allow none of these things. What I require is implicit submission, I look for nothing else but obedience to my law; as ye render not this but according to your own will, it is no worship of my name."

Prayer

Grant, Almighty God, that as thou wouldst have our
life to be formed by the rule of thy law, and hast there
revealed to us what pleaseth thee, that we may not
wander in uncertainty, but render thee obedience,—O
grant that we may wholly submit ourselves to thee,
and not only devote our whole life and all our labors to
thee, but also offer to thee as a sacrifice our
understanding and whatever prudence and reason we
possess, so that by spiritually serving thee we may
really glorify thy name, through Christ our Lord. Amen.

16

A Solemn Exhortation

Therefore thus will I do unto thee, O Israel: *and* because I will do this unto thee, prepare to meet thy God, O Israel. —Amos 4:12.

This passage may be explained in two ways; either as an ironical sentence, or as a simple and serious exhortation to repentance. If we take it ironically the sense will be, "Come now, meet me with all your obstinacy, and with whatever may serve you; will you be able to escape my vengeance by setting up yourselves against me, as you have hitherto done?" And certainly the prophet, in denouncing final ruin on the people, seems here as though he wished designedly to touch them to the quick, when he says, "Meet now thy God and prepare thyself;" that is, "Gather all thy strength and thy forces and thine auxiliaries; try what all this will avail thee." But as in the next chapter the prophet exhorts again the Israelites to repentance, and sets before them the hope of favor, this place may be taken in another sense, as though he said, "Since thou seest thyself guilty, and also as thou seest that thou art seeking subterfuges in vain, being not able by any means to elude the hand of thy judge, then see at last that thou meet thy God, that thou mayest anticipate the final ruin which is impending." The prophets, after having threatened destruction to the chosen people, ever moderate the asperity of their doctrine, as there were at all times some remnant seed, though hidden.

Prayer

Grant, Almighty God, that since by thy word thou kindly invitest us to thyself, we may not turn deaf ears to thee, but anticipate thy rod and scourges; and that when, for the stupidity and thoughtlessness by which we have become inebriated, thou addest those punishments by which thou sharply urgest us to repent,—O grant, that we may not continue wholly intractable, but at length turn our hearts to thy service and submit ourselves to the yoke of thy word, and that we may be so instructed by the punishments which thou hast inflicted on us and still inflictest, that we may truly and from the heart turn to thee, and offer ourselves to thee as a sacrifice, that thou mayest govern us according to thy will, and so rule all our affections by thy Spirit, that we may through the whole of our life strive to glorify thy name, in Christ Jesus, thy Son our Lord. Amen.

17

Herdman and Prophet

Then answered Amos, and said to Amaziah, 'I *was* no prophet, neither *was* I a prophet's son; but I *was* a herdman, and a gatherer of sycamore fruit.' —Amos 7:14.

Had Amos simply denied that he was a prophet, he might on this account have been thrust away from his office of teaching, for he lacked a call. But he means that he was not a prophet who had been from his childhood instructed in God's law to be an interpreter of Scripture: and for the same reason he says that he was not the son of a prophet; for there were then, we know, colleges for prophets, instituted for this end, that there might be always some nursery for the Church of God, so that it might not be destitute of good and faithful teachers. Amos says that he was not of that class. He therefore honestly confesses that he was an illiterate man: but by this he gained to himself more authority, inasmuch as the Lord had seized on him as it were by force, and set him over the people to teach them. It was a greater miracle that Christ chose rude and ignorant men as his apostles, than if he had at first chosen Paul or men like him, who were skilled in the law. If Christ had at the beginning selected such disciples their authority would have appeared less; but as he had prepared by his Spirit those who were before unlearned, it appeared more evident that they were sent from above.

Prayer

Grant, Almighty God, that inasmuch as thou dost give such loose reins to Satan, that he attempts in all manner of ways to subvert thy servants,—O grant, that they who have been sent and moved by thee and at the same time furnished with the invincible strength of thy Spirit may go on perseveringly to the last in the discharge of their office; and whether their adversaries assail them by plots or oppose them by open violence, may they not desist from their course but devote themselves wholly to thee with prudence as well as with courage that they may thus persevere in continual obedience: and do thou also dissipate all the mists and all the wiles which Satan spreads to deceive the inexperienced, until the truth emerge, which is the conqueror of the devil and of the whole world, and until thy Son, the Sun of Righteousness, appear, that he may gather the whole world that in his peaceful kingdom we may enjoy the victory, which is daily to be obtained by us in our constant struggles with the enemies of thine only Son. Amen.

18

The Power of God

It is he that buildeth his stories in the heaven, and hath founded his troop in the earth; he that calleth for the waters of the sea, and poureth them out upon the face of the earth: The LORD *is* his name.—Amos 9:6.

The prophet in general terms describes the power of God, that he might the more impress his hearers, and that they might not heedlessly reject what he had previously threatened respecting their approaching ruin; for he had said, "Lo, God will smite the land and it shall tremble." This was special. Now as men received with deaf ears those threatenings, the prophet added, by way of confirmation, a striking description of the power of God; as though he said, "Ye do hear what God denounces; now, as he has clothed me with his own authority, and commanded me to terrify you by setting before you your punishment, know ye that ye have to do with God himself, whose majesty ought to make you all and all that you are to tremble. Ye exist only through his power, and whenever he pleases he can withdraw his Spirit and then this whole world must vanish, of which ye are but the smallest particles. Since, then, he alone is God, and there is in you but a momentary strength, and since this great power of God, the evidences of which he affords you through the whole order of nature, is so conspicuous to you, how is it that ye are so heedless?"

Prayer

Grant, Almighty God, that as thou hast showed to us
by evidence so remarkable that all things are under
thy command, and that we who live in this world
through thy favor are as nothing, for thou couldst
reduce us to nothing in a moment,—O grant that
being conscious of thy power we may reverently fear
thy hand, and be wholly devoted to thy glory; and as
thou kindly offerest thyself to us as a Father, may we
be drawn by this kindness and surrender ourselves
wholly to thee by a willing obedience, and never labor
for anything through-out life but to glorify thy name
as thou hast redeemed us through thine only-
begotten Son, that so we may also enjoy through him
that eternal inheritance which is laid up for us in
heaven. Amen.

19

Wisdom Destroyed

Shall I not in that day, saith the LORD, even destroy the wise *men* out of Edom, and understanding out of the mount of Esau?— Obadiah 8.

Though men are in many respects blind, whom God guides not by his Spirit, and on whom he shines not with his word, yet the worst blindness is when men become inebriated with the false conceit of wisdom. God indeed permits the ungodly for a long time to felicitate themselves on account of their own acumen and counsels, as he suffered the Idumeans to go on prosperously. But we are warned by these words that if we excel in understanding, we are not to abuse this singular gift of God, as we see the case to be with the ungodly, who turn to cunning whatever wisdom the Lord has bestowed on them. There is hardly one in a hundred to be found who does not seek to be crafty and deceitful if he excels in understanding. We see that the world perverts this excellent gift of God; the more reason there is for us to labor, that our wisdom should be founded in true simplicity. This is one thing. Then we must also beware lest we trust in our own understanding and despise our enemies, and lest we think that we can ward off any evil that may impend over us; but let us ever seek from the Lord that he may vouchsafe to us at all times the Spirit of wisdom, that he may guide us even to the end of life.

Prayer

Grant, Almighty God, that as thou hast once for all received us under thy protection, and hast promised that our salvation would be so much under thy care, that whatever Satan and the whole world may contrive thou wilt yet keep us safe and secure,—O grant that being endued with perseverance, we may remain within our borders, and not be carried away here and there either by craft or by wicked counsels; but be thou pleased to keep us in genuine integrity; that, being protected by thy help, we may, by experience, find that true which thou declarest in thy word—that they who call on thee in truth shall ever know thee to be propitious to them; and since thou hast already made open to us an access to thee in the person of thine only-begotten Son, O grant that we, the sheep, may rely on him as our Shepherd, and resignedly abide under his protection until at length we be removed from all dangers into that eternal rest which has been obtained for us by the blood of Christ thine only Son. Amen.

20

A Fearless Preacher

And Jonah began to enter into the city a day's journey, and he cried, and said, 'Yet forty days, and Nineveh shall be overthrown.' — Jonah 3:4.

Jonah here relates that he went to Nineveh according to the command of God. He shows then how faithfully he executed the duty enjoined on him, and thus obeyed the word of God. Hence Jonah came and began to enter into the city, and to preach on the first day. This promptness proves clearly how tractable Jonah had become, and how much he endeavored to obey God in discharging his office. For had there been still a timidity in his heart, he would have inspected the city as careful and timid men are wont to do who inquire what is the condition of the place, what are the dispositions of the people, and which is the easiest access to them, and what is the best way and where is the least danger. We now see how prompt he was in his obedience who had before attempted to pass over the seas; he now takes hardly a moment to breathe, but he begins at the very entrance to testify that he had come in obedience to God.

He says that he cried; this freedom shows that Jonah was divested of all fear, and endued with such boldness of spirit that he raised himself up above all the hindrances of the world. No fear was able to prevent him from doing his duty as a faithful servant, for he had evidently been strengthened by the Lord.

Prayer

Grant, Almighty God, that as there is so much timidity in us that none of us is prepared to follow where thou mayest call us, we may be so instructed by the example of thy servant, Jonah, as to prepare ourselves for thorough obedience, and that though Satan and the world may oppose us with all their terrors, we may yet be strengthened by a reliance on thy power and protection, which thou hast promised to us, and may go on in the course of our vocation, and never turn aside, but thus contend with all the hindrances of this world, until we reach that celestial kingdom, where we shall enjoy thee, and Christ, thy only-begotten Son, who is our strength and our salvation; and may thy Spirit quicken us and strengthen all our faculties, that we may obey thee, and that at length thy name may be glorified in us, and that we may finally become partakers of that glory to which thou invitest us through Christ our only Lord. Amen.

21

The Mercy of God

Then said the LORD, 'Thou hast had pity on the gourd, for the which thou hast not labored, neither madest it grow; which came up in a night, and perished in a night: And should not I spare Nineveh, that great city, wherein are more than six-score thousand persons that cannot discern between their right hand and their left hand; and also much cattle?'—Jonah 4:10,11.

God shows here how like a father he provides for mankind. Each one of us is cherished by him with singular care; but yet he represents here a large number, that it might be more manifest that he has so great a concern for mankind that he will not inconsiderately fulminate against any one nation. God shows here to Jonah that he has been carried away by his own merciless zeal. Though his zeal arose from a good principle, yet Jonah was influenced by a feeling far too vehement. This God proved by sparing so many infants hitherto innocent. And to infants he adds the brute animals. Oxen were certainly superior to shrubs. If Jonah justly grieved for one withered shrub it was far more deplorable and cruel for so many innocent animals to perish. We hence see how apposite are all the parts of this similitude, to make Jonah loathe his folly, and to be ashamed of it; for he had attempted to frustrate the secret purpose of God, and in a manner to overrule it by his own will, so that the Ninevites might not be spared, although they labored by true repentance to anticipate the divine judgment.

Prayer

Grant, Almighty God, that as thou hast, in various ways, testified and daily also dost prove how dear and precious to thee are mankind, as we enjoy daily so many and so remarkable proofs of thy goodness and favor,—O grant that we may learn to rely wholly on thy goodness, so many examples of which thou settest before us, and which thou wouldst have us continually to experience, that we may not only pass through our earthly course, but also confidently aspire to the hope of that blessed and celestial life which is laid up for us in heaven, through Christ alone our Lord. Amen.

22

A Prophet's Lamentation

For her wound is incurable; for it is come unto Judah; he is come unto the gate of my people, *even* to Jerusalem. —Micah 1:9.

The prophet here assumed the character of a mourner that he might more deeply impress the Israelites; for they were almost insensible in their torpidity. It was therefore necessary that they should be brought to view the scene itself, that, seeing their destruction before their eyes, they might be touched both with grief and fear. Though the prophet here addresses the Israelites, we ought yet to apply this to ourselves; for we are not much unlike the ancient people: for however God may terrify us with dreadful threatenings, we still remain quiet. It is therefore needful that we should be severely treated, for we are almost void of feeling. The prophet does here these two things, he shows the fraternal love which he entertained for the children of Israel, as they were his kindred and a part of the chosen people,—and he also discharges his own duty; for this lamentation was, as it were, the mirror in which he sets before them the vengeance of God toward men so extremely torpid. He therefore exhibits to them this representation that they might perceive that God was by no means trifling with men, when he thus denounced punishment on the wicked and such as were apostates.

Prayer

Grant, Almighty God, that being warned by so many examples, the record of which thou hast designed to continue to the end of the world, that we may learn how dreadful a judge thou art, to the perverse,—O grant, that we may not at this day, be hardened against thy teaching which is conveyed to us by the mouth of thy prophet, but that we may strive to be so reconciled to thee, that, passing by all men, we may present ourselves unreservedly to thee, so that, relying on thy mercy alone, which thou hast promised to us in Christ, we may not doubt that thou wilt be propitious to us, and be so touched with the spirit of true penitence, that if we have been to others a bad example, and offense, we may lead others to the right way of salvation, and each of us may so endeavor to assist our neighbors in a holy life, that we may together attain that blessed and celestial life which thine only-begotten Son has procured for us by his own blood. Amen.

23

Strengthened by the Spirit

But truly I am full of power by the spirit of the LORD, and of judgment, and of might, to declare unto Jacob his transgression, and to Israel his sin.—Micah 3:8.

Here Micah, in a courageous spirit, stands up alone against all the false teachers, even when he saw that they were a large number, and that they appealed to their number, according to their usual practice, as their shield. This confidence is what all God's servants should possess, that they may not succumb to the empty and vain boastings of those who subvert the whole order of the Church. Whenever, then, God permits his pure truth to be corrupted by false teachers and allows them to be popular among those high in honor, as well as with the multitude, let this striking example be remembered by us lest we be discouraged, lest the firmness and invincible power of the Holy Spirit be weakened in our hearts; but let us proceed in the course of our calling and learn to oppose the name of God to all the deceptions of men, if indeed we are convinced that our service is approved by him as being faithful. Micah no doubt shows here, on account of the necessity of the occasion, that he was not supplied with ordinary or usual power; for, according as God employs the labors of his servants, so is he present with them, and furnishes them with suitable protection.

Prayer

Grant, Almighty God, that as thou wouldst have us to be ruled by the preaching of thy word,—O grant that those who have to discharge this office may be really endued with thy celestial power that they may not attempt anything of themselves, but with all devotedness spend all their labors for thee and for our benefit, that through them we may be thus edified so that thou mayest ever dwell among us, and that we through our whole life may become the habitation of thy majesty, and that finally we may come to thy heavenly sanctuary, where thou daily invitest us, as an entrance there has been once for all opened to us by the blood of thine only-begotten Son. Amen.

24

A Fellowship of Nations

And many nations shall come, and say, 'Come, and let us go up to the mountain of the LORD, and to the house of the God of Jacob; and he will teach us of his ways, and we will walk in his paths:' for the law shall go forth of Zion, and the word of the Lord from Jerusalem. —Micah 4:2.

The prophet shows in these words, that not only each one would be obedient to God, when called, but that they would also encourage one another; and this ardor is what is justly required in the faithful; they ought to animate and urge on one another; for it is not enough for each of us himself to obey God, but this zeal ought to be added, by which we may strive to produce a mutual benefit. The manner of the exhortation deserves to be noticed; for each one offers himself as a companion in the journey. We see indeed that many are prompt enough when others are to be stimulated in their duty; but they at the same time lie still; their whole fervor is consumed in sending others, and they themselves move not, no, not a finger; so far are they from running with alacrity in company with others. The prophet shows here that the faithful will be so solicitous about the salvation of their brethren that they themselves also will strenuously run, and that they will prescribe nothing to others but what they themselves perform.

Prayer

Grant, Almighty God, that since, at the coming of Christ thy Son thou didst really perform what thy servants the prophets had foretold so long before, and since thou daily invitest us until now to the unity of faith, that with united efforts we may truly serve thee,—O grant, that we may not continue torn asunder, every one pursuing his own perverse inclinations, at a time when Christ is thus gathering us unto thee; nor let us only profess with the mouth and in words that we are under thy government, but prove that we feel this very thing in real sincerity; and may we then add to the true and lawful worship of thy name brotherly love toward one another, that with united efforts we may promote each other's good, and that our adoption may thus be proved and be more and more confirmed that we may ever be able with full confidence to call on thee as our Father, through Christ our Lord. Amen.

25
The Constancy of Faith

For all people will walk every one in the name of his god, and we will walk in the name of the LORD our God for ever and ever.
—Micah 4:5

Micah, after having spoken of the restoration of the Church, now confirms the same truth, and shows that the faithful would have reason enough to cleave constantly to their God, and to despise all the superstitions of the world, and that though they may be tossed here and there by contrary opinions, they will yet continue in true piety. This verse, then, is connected with the kingdom of Christ, for until we are gathered, and Christ shines among us and rules us by his word, there can be in us no constancy, no firmness. But when, under the auspices of Christ, we join together in one body, the Church, such then becomes the constancy of our faith that nothing can turn us aside from the right course, though new storms were at any time to arise, by which the whole world might be shaken, and though it were to happen that the universe should pass away.

This passage shows that faith depends not on the suffrages of men, and that we ought not to regard what any one may think, or what may be the consent of all, for the truth of God alone ought to be deemed sufficient by us. How much soever, then, the whole world may oppose God, our faith ought not to be changeable, but remain firm on this foundation—that God, who cannot deceive, hath spoken.

Prayer

Grant, Almighty God, that since under the guidance of thy Son we have been united together in the body of thy Church, which has been so often scattered and torn asunder,—O grant that we may continue in the unity of faith, and perseveringly fight against all the temptations of this world, and never deviate from the right course, whatever new troubles may daily arise; and though we are exposed to many deaths, let us not be seized with fear, such as may extinguish in our hearts every hope; but may we, on the contrary, learn to raise up our eyes and minds and all our thoughts to thy great power, by which thou quickenest the dead, and raisest from nothing things which are not, so that, though we be daily exposed to ruin, our souls may ever aspire to eternal salvation, until thou at length really showest thyself to be the fountain of life, when we shall enjoy that endless felicity which has been obtained for us by the blood of thine only-begotten Son our Lord. Amen.

26
God's Requirements

He hath showed thee, O man, what *is* good; and what doth the LORD require of thee, but to do justly, and to love mercy, and to walk humbly with thy God?—Micah 6:8.

It is evident that, in the first two particulars, he refers to the second table of the law; that is, to do justice and to love mercy. Nor is it a matter of wonder that the prophet begins with the duties of love; for though in rank the worship of God precedes these duties and ought rightly to be so regarded, yet justice, which is to be exercised toward men, is the real evidence of religion. The prophet, therefore, mentions justice and mercy, not that God casts aside what is first in importance,—the worship of his name; but he shows by evidences or effects, what true religion is. He afterwards adds what in order is first, and that is, literally, "to be humble in walking with thy God." No doubt as the name of God is more excellent than anything else in the whole world, so the worship of him ought to be regarded as of more importance than all those duties by which we prove our love toward men. But the prophet, as I have already said, was not so particular in observing order. His main object was to show how men were to prove that they seriously feared God and kept his law; he afterwards speaks of God's worship. But his manner of speaking, when he says, that men ought to be humble, that they may walk with their God, is worthy of special notice.

Prayer

Grant, Almighty God, that as thou hast made known to us thy law, and hast also added thy gospel, in which thou callest us to thy service, and also invitest us with all kindness to partake of thy grace,—O grant, that we may not be deaf, either to thy command or to the promises of thy mercy, but render ourselves submissive to thee everywhere, and so learn to devote all our faculties to thee, that we may in truth avow that the rule of a holy and religious life, has been delivered to us in thy law, and that we may firmly adhere to thy promises, lest through any of the allurements of the world, or through the flatteries and delusions of Satan, thou shouldst suffer our minds to be drawn away from that love which thou hast once for all manifested to us in thine only-begotten Son, and in which thou daily confirmest its by the teaching of the gospel, until we at length shall come to the full enjoyment of this love in that celestial inheritance, which has been purchased for us by the blood of thine only Son. Amen.

27

A Prayer for God's Heritage

Feed thy people with thy rod, the flock of thine heritage, which dwell solitarily *in* the wood, in the midst of Carmel: let them feed *in* Bashan and Gilead, as in the days of old.—Micah 7:14.

The prophet here turns to supplications and prayers, by which he manifests more vehemence than if he had affirmed what he had previously said of the restoration of the Church; for he shows how dreadful that judgment would be when God would reduce the land into a solitude. This prayer no doubt contains what was at the same time prophetic. He compares God to a shepherd, and this metaphor often occurs. By calling them the flock of his heritage, he does not consider what the people deserved, but fixes his eyes on their gratuitous adoption. Since, then, it had pleased God to choose that people, the prophet on this account dares to go forth to God's presence and to plead their gratuitous election,—"O Lord, I will not bring before thee the nobility of our race, or any sort of dignity, or our piety, or any merits." What then? "We are thy people, for thou hast declared that we are a royal priesthood. We are accordingly thy heritage." How so? "Because it has been thy pleasure to have one peculiar people sacred to thee." We now more clearly see that the prophet relied on God's favor alone, and opposed the recollection of the covenant to the trials which might have otherwise made every hope to fail.

Prayer

Grant, Almighty God, that since we have so provoked thy displeasure by our sins, that a dreadful waste and solitude appear everywhere,—O grant that a proof of that favor which thou hast so remarkably exhibited toward thine ancient people may shine upon us, so that thy Church may be raised up in which true religion may flourish, and thy name be glorified; and may we daily solicit thee in our prayers, and never doubt that under the government of thy Christ thou canst again gather together the whole world, though it be miserably dispersed, so that we may persevere in this warfare to the end, until we shall at length know that we have not in vain hoped in thee, and that our prayers have not been in vain, when Christ evidently shall exercise the power given to him for our salvation and for that of the whole world. Amen.

28

Nineveh's Fall

But Nineveh is of old like a pool of water: yet they shall flee away. Stand, O stand, *shall they cry;* but none shall look back.—Nahum 2:8.

The prophet here anticipates a doubt which might have weakened confidence in his words, for Nineveh not only flourished in power, but it had also confirmed its strength during a long course of time; and antiquity not only adds to the strength of kingdoms, but secures authority to them. Accordingly, as the imperial city of Nineveh was ancient, it might even seem to have been perpetual. "Why! Nineveh has ever ruled and possessed the sovereign power in all the East. Can it be now shaken, or can its strength be now suddenly subverted? For where there is no beginning we cannot believe that there will be any end." The Ninevites, no doubt, boasted that they had been eternal, and as they were fixed in this conceit concerning their antiquity, no one thought they could ever fail. This circumstance shall not, however, prevent God from now overturning its dominion. How much soever, then, Nineveh took pride in the notion of its ancientness, it was yet God's purpose to destroy it. From this passage we ought to learn that no trust is to be put in the number of men, nor in the defenses and strong-holds of cities, nor in ancientness; for when men excel in power God will hence take occasion to destroy them, inasmuch as pride is almost always connected with strength.

Prayer

Grant, Almighty God, that as thou constantly remindest us in thy word, and hast taught us by so many examples, that there is nothing permanent in this world, but that the things which seem the firmest tend to ruin, and instantly fall and of themselves vanish away, when by thy breath thou shakest that strength in which men trust,—O grant that we, being really subdued and humbled, may not rely on earthly things, but raise up our hearts and our thoughts to heaven, and there fix the anchor of our hope; and may all our thoughts abide there until at length, when thou hast led us through our course on earth, we shall be gathered into that celestial kingdom which has been obtained for us by the blood of thine only-begotten Son. Amen.

29

The Watch Tower

I will stand upon my watch, and set me upon the tower, and will watch to see what he will say unto me, and what I shall answer when I am reproved.—Habakkuk 2:1.

The prophet finding himself sinking, and as it were overwhelmed in the deepest abyss, raises himself up above the judgment and reason of men, and comes nearer to God, that he might see from on high the things which take place on earth, and not judge according to the understanding of his own flesh but by the light of the Holy Spirit. For the tower of which he speaks is patience arising from hope. If we contend with Satan according to our own view of things, he will a hundred times overwhelm us, and we can never be able to resist him. Let us therefore know that here is shown to us the right way of fighting with him. When our minds are agitated with unbelief, when things are so confused in this world as to involve us in darkness, so that no light appears: we must bid adieu to our own reason; for all our thoughts are worth nothing, when we seek, according to our own reason, to form a judgment. Consequently until the faithful ascend to their tower and stand in their citadel, of which the prophet here speaks, their temptations will drive them here and there, and sink them as it were in a bottomless gulf. The tower is the recess of the mind; but how can we ascend to it? Even by following the word of the Lord.

Prayer

Grant, Almighty God, that as thou seest us laboring under so much weakness, yea, with our minds so blinded that our faith falters at the smallest perplexities, and almost fails altogether,—O grant, that by the power of thy Spirit we may be raised up above this world, and learn more and more to renounce our own counsels, and so to come to thee, that we may stand fixed in our watch tower, ever hoping through thy power, for whatever thou hast promised us, though thou shouldst not immediately make it manifest to us, that thou hast faithfully spoken; and may we thus give full proof of our faith and patience, and proceed in the course of our warfare, until at length we ascend above all watch towers into that blessed rest where we shall no more watch with an attentive mind, but, see face to face, in thine image, whatever can be wished, and whatever is needful for our perfect happiness through Christ our Lord. Amen.

30

Punishment for Avarice

Shall not all these take up a parable against him, and a taunting proverb against him, and say, 'Woe to him that increaseth *that which is* not his! how long? and to him that ladeth himself with thick clay!'
—Habakkuk 2:6

All the people who had been collected, as it were, into a heap, would take up a parable or taunt in order to scoff at the king of Babylon. What seems here to be the singing of triumph before the victory is no matter of wonder, for our faith, as it is well known, depends not on the judgment of the flesh, nor regards what is openly evident, but it is the substance of things hoped for, and the evidence of things not seen (Heb. 11:1). As then, the firmness of faith is the same, though what it apprehends is remote, and as faith ceaseth not to see things hidden—for through the mirror of God's word it ascends above heaven and earth, and penetrates into the spiritual kingdom of God—as faith, then, possesses a view so distant, it is not to be wondered that the prophet here boldly triumphs over the Babylonians and now prescribes a derisive song for all nations. The prophet also intimates that tyrants and their cruelty cannot be endured without great weariness and sorrow; hence, almost the whole world sound forth these words, 'How long?' And this feeling, is it not implanted in us by the Lord? But let us in the mean time see that no one of us should say the same thing to himself which he brings forward against others.

Prayer

Grant Almighty God, that as thou deignest so far to condescend as to sustain the care of this life, and to supply us with whatever is needful for our pilgrimage,—O grant that we may learn also to rely on thee and so trust to thy blessing as to abstain not only from all plunder and all other evil deeds, but also from every unlawful coveting; and to continue in thy fear, and so to learn also to bear our poverty on the earth, that being content with those spiritual riches, which thou offerest to us in thy gospel, and of which thou makest us now partakers, we may ever cheerfully aspire after that fullness of all blessings, which we shall enjoy when at length we shall reach the celestial kingdom and be perfectly united to thee through Christ our Lord. Amen.

31

Chariots of Salvation

Was the Lord displeased against the rivers? *was* thine anger against the rivers? *was* thy wrath against the sea, that thou didst ride upon thine horses *and* thy chariots of salvation?—Habakkuk 3:8.

A question has much more force when it refers to what is in no way doubtful. What! Can God be angry with rivers? Who can imagine God to be so unreasonable as to disturb the sea and to change the nature of things, when a certain order has been established by his own command? Why should he dry the sea, unless he had something in view, even the deliverance of his Church? Unless he intended to save his people from extreme danger by stretching forth his hand to the Israelites when they thought themselves utterly lost? He therefore denies that when God dried the Red Sea, and when he stopped the flowing of Jordan, he had put forth his power against the sea or against the river as though he were angry with them. The design of God, says the prophet, was quite another; for God rode on his horses, that is, he intended to show that all the elements were under his command, and that for the salvation of his people. That God, then, might be the redeemer of his Church, he constrained the Jordan to turn back its course, he constrained the Red Sea to make a passage for his miserable captives, who would otherwise have been exposed, as it were, to slaughter.

Prayer

Grant, Almighty God, that as thou hast so often and in such various ways testified formerly, how much care and solicitude thou hast for the salvation of all those who may rely and call on thee,—O grant, that we also at this day may experience the same, and though thy face is justly hid from us, may we yet never hesitate to flee to thee since thou hast made a covenant through thy Son, which is founded in thine infinite mercy; grant, then, that we, being humbled in true penitence, may so surrender ourselves to thy Son, that we may be led to thee, and find thee no less a Father to us than to the faithful of old, as thou everywhere testifiest to us in thy word, until at length, being freed from all troubles and dangers, we come to that blessed rest which thine only Son has purchased for us by his own blood. Amen.

32

Rejoicing in the Lord

Although the fig tree shall not blossom, neither *shall* fruit *be* in the vines; the labor of the olive shall fail, and the fields shall yield no meat; the flock shall be cut off from the fold, and *there shall be* no herd in the stalls: Yet I will rejoice in the LORD, I will joy in the God of my salvation. —Habakkuk 3:17,18

The prophet teaches us what advantage it is to the faithful seasonably to submit to God and to entertain serious fear when he threatens them and when he summons them to judgment; and he shows that though they might perish a hundred times, they would yet not perish, for the Lord would ever supply them with occasions of joy, and would also cherish this joy within, so as to enable them to rise above all their adversities. Though the land was threatened with the famine, and though no food would be supplied to them, they would yet be able always to rejoice in the God of their salvation; for they knew him to be their Father, though for a time he severely chastised them. Our joy shall not depend on outward prosperity, for though the Lord may afflict us in an extreme degree, there will yet always be some consolations to sustain our minds that they may not succumb under evils so grievous, for we are fully persuaded that our salvation is in God's hand, and that he is its faithful guardian. We shall, therefore, rest quietly; yea, though God fulminated from heaven we shall yet be in a tranquil state of mind, looking for his gratuitous salvation.

Prayer

Grant, Almighty God, that as we cease not daily to provoke thy wrath against us, and as the hardness and obstinacy of our flesh is so great that it is necessary for us to be in various ways afflicted,—O grant that we may patiently bear thy chastisements, and under a deep feeling of sorrow flee to thy mercy; and may we in the mean time persevere in the hope of that mercy, which thou hast promised, and which has once for all been exhibited toward us in Christ, so that we may not depend on the earthly blessings of this perishable life, but, relying on thy word, may proceed in the course of our calling until we shall at length be gathered into that blessed rest which is laid up for us in heaven, through Christ alone our Lord. Amen.

33

Pride and Destruction

This is the rejoicing city that dwelt carelessly, that said in her heart, 'I *am*, and *there is* none beside me:' how is she become a desolation, a place for beasts to lie down in! every one that passeth by her shall hiss, *and* wag his hand.—Zephaniah 2:15.

The prophet reminds them here that though Nineveh was thus proud of its wealth, yet it could not escape the hand of God; nay, he shows that the greatness, on account of which Nineveh extolled itself, would be the cause of its ruin; for it would cast itself down by its own pride, as a wall when it swells will not stand. Such a destruction the prophet denounces on the Ninevites and the Assyrians. Let us remember that in this city is presented to us an example which belongs in common to all nations,—that God cannot endure the presumption of men, when inflated by their own greatness and power they do not think themselves to be men, nor humble themselves in a way suitable to the conditions of men, but forget themselves, as though they could exalt themselves above the heavens. If, then, we desire to be protected by God's hand, let us bear in mind what our condition is, and daily, yea hourly, prepare ourselves for a change, except God be pleased to sustain us. Our stability is to depend only on the aid of God, and from consciousness of our infirmity to tremble in ourselves lest a fearfulness of our state should creep in.

Prayer

Grant, Almighty God, that as thou triest us in the warfare of the cross, and arousest most powerful enemies whose barbarity might justly terrify and dishearten us, were we not depending on thine aid,—O grant, that we may call to mind how wonderfully thou didst in former times deliver thy people, and how seasonably thou didst bring them help, when they were oppressed and entirely overwhelmed, so that we may learn at this day to flee to thy protection, and not doubt, that when thou becomest propitious to us there is in thee sufficient power to preserve us, and to lay prostrate our enemies, how much soever they may now exult and think to triumph above the heavens, so that they may at length know by experience that they are earthly and frail creatures, whose life and condition is like the mist which soon vanishes; and may we learn to aspire after that blessed eternity which is laid up for us in heaven through Christ our Lord. Amen.

34

Pure Lips

For then will I turn to the people a pure language that they may all call upon the name of the LORD, to serve him with one consent.
—Zephaniah 3:9

God intimates that he would propagate his grace wider after having cleansed the earth, for he will be worshiped not only in Judea, but by foreign nations, and even by the remotest. God has in his own hand the means by which he will vindicate his own glory; for he will not only defend his Church in Judea, but will also gather into it nations far and wide, so that his name shall be everywhere celebrated. God does not without reason promise that he will turn pure lips to the nations—that is, that lie will cause the nations to call on his name with pure lips. We hence learn that God cannot rightly be invoked by us until he draws us to himself, for we have profane and impure lips. As to the word "all," it is to be referred to nations, not to each individual, for it has not been brought to pass that every one has called on God; but there have been some of all nations, as Paul also says in the first chapter of the first Epistle to the Corinthians, for in addressing the faithful he adds, "With all that in every place call upon the name of Jesus Christ our Lord, both theirs and ours"—that is, not only in Judea; and elsewhere he says, "I will that men pray everywhere, lifting up holy hands, without wrath and doubting" (1 Timothy 2:8).

Prayer

Grant, Almighty God, that since it is the principal part of our happiness that while we are absent from thee in this world there is yet open to us a familiar access to thee by faith,—O grant that we may be able to come with a pure heart to thy presence; and when our lips are polluted, O purify us by thy Spirit, so that we may not only pray to thee with the mouth, but also prove that we do this sincerely, without any dissimulation, and that we earnestly seek to spend our whole life in glorifying thy name, until at length being gathered into thy celestial kingdom, we may be really and truly united to thee, and be made partakers of that glory which has been procured for us by the blood of thine only Son. Amen.

35

Uses of Affliction

I will also leave in the midst of thee an afflicted and poor people, and they shall trust in the name of the LORD. —Zephaniah 3:12

It ought to have been a compensation to ease their grief, when the godly saw that God would be propitious to them, though he had treated them with great severity. The Church could not have been preserved without correcting and subduing that arrogance, which arose from a false profession as to God. Zephaniah takes it now for granted that pride could not be torn away from their hearts, unless they were wholly cast down and thus made contrite. The Church is subdued by the cross, that she may know her pride, which is so innate and so fixed in the hearts of men that it cannot be removed, unless the Lord, so to speak, roots it out by force. There is, therefore, no wonder that the faithful are so much humbled by the Lord, and that the lot of the Church is so contemptible; for if they had more vigor they would soon, as is often the case, break out into an insolent spirit. We hence see for what purpose God deprives us of all earthly trust, and takes away from us every ground of glorying; it is, that we rely only on his favor. This dependence ought not, indeed, to be extorted from us, for what can be more desirable than to trust in God? But while men arrogate to themselves more than what is right, and thus put themselves in the place of God, they cannot really and sincerely trust in him.

Prayer

Grant, Almighty God, that since the depravity of our nature is so great that we cannot bear prosperity without some wantonness of the flesh immediately raging in us, and without becoming even arrogant against thee,—O grant that we may profit under the trials of the cross, and when thou humblest us, may we with lowly hearts renouncing our perverseness, submit ourselves to thee, and not only bear thy yoke submissively, but proceed in this obedience through all our life, and so contend against all temptations, as never to glory in ourselves, and feel also convinced that all true and real glory is laid up for us in thee, until we shall enjoy it in thy celestial kingdom, through Christ our Lord. Amen.

36

A Mirror for Ingratitude

Thus speaketh the LORD of hosts, saying, "This people say, 'The time is not come, the time that the LORD'S house should be built'."—Haggai 1:2.

We may see here, as in a mirror, how great the ingratitude of men is. The kindness of God had been especially worthy of being remembered, the glory of which ought to have been borne in mind to the end of time. They had been restored from exile in a manner beyond what they had ever expected. What ought they to have done, but devote themselves entirely to the service of their deliverer? But they built, no, not even a tent for God, and sacrificed in the open air; and thus they willfully trifled with God. But at the same time they dwelt at ease in houses elegantly fitted up. No less shameful is the example witnessed at this day among us.

But we may hence also see how kindly God has provided for his Church; for his purpose was that this reproof should continue extant, that he might at this day stimulate us, and excite our fear as well as our shame. For we also thus grow frigid in promoting the worship of God whenever we are led to seek our own advantages. We may also add that as God's temple is spiritual, our fault is the more atrocious when we become thus slothful; since God does not bid us to collect either wood, or stones, or cement, but to build a celestial temple in which he may be truly worshiped.

Prayer

Grant, Almighty God, that as we must carry on a
warfare in this world, and as it is thy will to try us with
many contests,—O grant that we may never faint,
however extreme may be the trials which we may have
to endure; and as thou hast favored us with so great
an honor as to make us the framers and builders of
thy spiritual temple, may every one of us present and
consecrate himself wholly to thee; and inasmuch as
each of us has received some peculiar gift, may we
strive to employ it in building this temple, so that thou
mayest be worshiped among us perpetually; and
especially may each of us offer himself wholly as a
spiritual sacrifice to thee, until we shall at length be
renewed in thine image, and be received into a full
participation of that glory which has been attained for
us by the blood of thine only-begotten Son. Amen.

37

A Glorious Temple

'The silver *is* mine, and the gold *is mine,'* saith the LORD of hosts.
—Haggai 2:8.

Why does the prophet mention gold and silver? He did this in conformity with what was usual and common, for whenever the prophets speak of the kingdom of Christ they delineate or foreshadow its splendor in figurative terms, suitable to their own age. When Isaiah foretells the restoration of the Church he declares that the Church would be all gold and silver, and whatever glittered with precious stones; and in the sixtieth chapter he especially sets forth the magnificence of the temple, as though nations from all parts were to bring for sacrifice all their precious things. Isaiah speaks figuratively, as all the other prophets do. But we must regard the spiritual character of the priesthood, for since Christ has appeared in the world it is not God's will to be served with gold and silver vessels; so, also, there is no altar on which victims are to be sacrificed, and no candlestick; in a word, all the symbols of the law have ceased. Thus we perceive how the glory of the second temple is to be greater than that of the first. For though they were to gather the treasures of a thousand worlds into one mass, such a glory would yet be corruptible; but when God the Father appeared in the person of his own Son, he so glorified his temple that there was nothing wanting to a complete perfection.

Prayer

Grant, Almighty God, that since we are by nature extremely prone to superstition, we may carefully consider what is the true and right way of serving thee, such as thou dost desire and approve even that we offer ourselves spiritually to thee, and seek no other altar but Christ, and relying on no other priest, hope to be acceptable and devoted to thee, that he may imbue us with the Spirit which has been fully poured on him so that we may from the heart devote ourselves to thee, and thus proceed patiently in our course, that with minds raised upward we may ever go on toward that glory which is as yet hid under hope until it shall at length be manifested in his own time, when thine only-begotten Son shall appear with the elect angels for our final redemption. Amen.

38

Abundant Blessing

Consider now from this day and upward, from the four and twentieth day of the ninth *month, even* from the day that the foundation of the LORD'S temple was laid, consider *it.*

Is the seed yet in the barn? Yea, as yet the vine, and the fig tree, and the pomegranate, and the olive tree, hath not brought forth: from this day will I bless *you.*—Haggai 2:18,19.

The "seed" refers not to what had been gathered, but to what had been sown. The prophet speaks of God's blessing on the harvest which was to come. As they were still in suspense, he says that God's blessing was in readiness for them. The truth of the prophecy might be truly known when God fulfilled what he had spoken by the mouth of his servant. It was necessary for him to speak in a manner suitable to the comprehension of the people, as a skillful teacher who instructs children and those of a riper age in a different manner. The prophet dwells on two things: he condemns the Jews for their neglect, and proves that they were impious and ungrateful toward God, for they disregarded the building of the temple; and then in order to animate them and render them more active in the work they had begun, he sets before them what had taken place.

Prayer

Grant, Almighty God, that as we are still restrained by our earthly cares, and cannot ascend upward to heaven with so much readiness and alacrity as we ought,—O grant that since thou extendest to us daily so liberal a supply for the present life, we may at least learn that thou art our Father, and that we may not at the same time fix our thoughts on these perishable things, but learn to elevate our minds higher, and so make continual advances in thy spiritual service until at length we come to the full and complete fruition of that blessed and celestial life which thou hast promised to us, and procured for us by the blood of thy only-begotten Son. Amen.

39

Horns and Carpenters

Then lifted I up mine eyes, and saw, and behold four horns. And I said unto the angel that talked with me, 'What *be* these?' And he answered me, 'These *are* the horns which have scattered Judah, Israel, and Jerusalem.' And the LORD showed me four carpenters. Then said I, 'What come these to do?' And he spake, saying, 'These *are* the horns which have scattered Judah, so that no man did lift up his head: but these are come to fray them, to cast out the horns of the Gentiles, which lifted up *their* horn over the land of Judah to scatter it.'—Zechariah 1:18-21.

Though enemies should rise up on every side against the Church and cause it many troubles, there was yet a remedy in God's hand, as he would break in pieces all horns by his hammers. He compares the Gentiles, who had been hostile to the Jews, to horns; and he afterwards compares to workmen the other enemies, whose hand and labor God would use for the purpose of breaking down the efforts of all those who would be troublesome to the Church. The import of the whole then is—that though the Church would not be exempt and free from many troubles, yet God would have in his hand those remedies by which he would check all the assaults of the wicked. Though the prophet intended by this prophecy to encourage and animate to patience his own nation, yet there is here set before us by the Lord, as in a mirror, the real condition of the Church at this day.

Prayer

Grant, Almighty God that as we are on every side surrounded by many enemies and as Satan never ceases to kindle the fury of many, not only to be hostile to us, but also to destroy and consume us,—O grant that we may learn to raise up our eyes to heaven, and trusting in thy protection may boldly fight in patience, until at length that shall appear which thou hast once for all testified in this remarkable prophecy, that there are many smiths in thine hand and also many hammers, by which thou breakest in pieces those horns which rise up to scatter us, and until at length having overcome all the devices of Satan, we shall reach that blessed rest which has been provided for us by the blood of thine only-begotten Son. Amen.

40

The True Priest

And he showed me Joshua the high priest standing before the angel of the LORD, and Satan standing at his right hand to resist him.
—Zechariah 3:1.

Zechariah labored to show that the faithful were to look for more than they had reason to expect from the aspect of things at the time, and that they were to direct their eyes and their thoughts to the power of God, which was not as yet manifested, and which indeed God purposely designed not to exercise, in order to try the patience of the people. The vision was given to the prophet for two reasons—that the faithful might know that their contest was with Satan, their spiritual enemy, rather than with neighboring nations, and also that they might understand that a remedy was at hand, for God stood in defense of the priesthood which he had instituted. That typical priesthood was a representation of the priesthood of Christ, and Joshua, who was then returned from exile, bore the character of Christ the Son of God. Let us then know that Christ never performs the work of the priesthood, but that Satan stands at his side—that is, devises all means by which he may remove and draw Christ from his office. It hence follows that they are much deceived who think that they can live idly under the dominion of Christ, for we all have a warfare, for which each is to arm and equip himself. Let not our thoughts be fixed on flesh and blood, for Satan is the chief warrior who assails us.

Prayer

Grant, Almighty God, that as thou hast made us a royal priesthood in thy Son, that we may daily offer to thee spiritual sacrifices, and be devoted to thee both in body and soul,—O grant that we, being endued with thy power, may boldly fight against Satan, and never doubt that thou wilt finally give us the victory, though we may have to undergo many troubles and difficulties; and may not the contempt of the world frighten or dishearten us, but may we patiently bear all our reproaches until thou at length stretchest forth thy hand to raise us up to that glory, the perfection of which now appears in our Head, and shall at last be clearly seen in all the members, and in the whole body, even when he shall come to gather us into that celestial kingdom which he has purchased for us by his own blood. Amen.

41

The Day of Small Things

For who hath despised the day of small things? For they shall rejoice, and shall see the plummet in the hand of Zerubbabel *with* those seven; they *are* the eyes of the LORD, which run to and fro through the whole earth.—Zechariah 4:10.

God, to exhibit the more his power, begins with small things in building his spiritual temple; nothing grand is seen to attract the eyes and thoughts of men, but everything is almost contemptible. God indeed could put forth his power immediately, and thus rouse the attention of all men and fill them with wonder. But his purpose is to increase, by doing wonders, the brightness of his power, which he does when from a small beginning he brings forth what no one would have thought; and besides, his purpose is to prove the faith of his people, for it behooves us ever to hope beyond hope. Now, when the beginning promises something great and sublime, there is no proof and no trial of faith; but when we hope for what does not appear, we give due honor to God, for we depend only on his power, and not on the proximate means. There is no one who does not sometimes become cold when he sees the beginning of the Church so mean before the world and so destitute of any dignity. But we know that Christ is the chief builder and that ministers are workmen who labor under him.

Prayer

Grant, Almighty God, that since Satan at this day sets against us many terrors to cast us down, and we are very weak,—O grant that with our eyes lifted above we may meditate on that invincible power which thou possessest, and by which thou canst overcome all the hindrances of this world, and then, when nothing in this world but what is contemptible appears to be capable of confirming and supporting our faith, may we, nevertheless, by the eyes of faith, behold thy hidden power and never doubt that thou wilt at length perform what the world at this day thinks to be impossible, and therefore ridicules; and may we so constantly persevere in this confidence that every one of us may devote to thee his labor to the end, and never faint in the work of promoting the spiritual building, until at length we ourselves shall be assembled, and others also shall be gathered through our labors, to offer to thee not only spiritual sacrifices such as thou receivest now from us, but also to offer to thee, together with the angels, that eternal sacrifice of praise and triumphant thanksgiving on seeing perfected what at this day is only feebly begun. Amen

42

The Providence of God

Then cried he upon me, and spake unto me saying, 'Behold, these that go toward the North Country have quieted my spirit in the North Country.'—Zechariah 6:8.

From this verse we learn that the chief object of the vision was, that the Jews might know that the dreadful tumults in Chaldea, which had in part happened, and were yet to take place, were not excited without a design; but that all things were regulated by God's hidden counsel, and also that God had so disturbed and embarrassed the state of that empire that the end of it might be looked for. There is, therefore, no reason for any one too anxiously to labor to understand the import of every part of the prophecy, since its general meaning is evident. But why does the angel expressly speak of the land of the south rather than of the land of the north, or of the whole world? Even because the eyes of all were fixed on that quarter; for Chaldea, we know, had been, as it were, the grave of the Church, whence the remnant had emerged, that there might be some people by whom God might be worshiped. The angel then bids the Jews to continue undisturbed in their minds, until these chariots had run their course through the whole of Chaldea; for what the angel now says would be fulfilled, even that the Spirit of God would be quieted, who seemed before to be disturbed when he involved all things in darkness, even in Judea itself.

Prayer

Grant, Almighty God, that since we are here exposed to so many evils, which suddenly arise like violent tempests,—O grant, that with hearts raised up to heaven, we may yet acquiesce in thy hidden providence, and be so tossed here and there, according to the judgment of our flesh, as yet to remain fixed in this truth, which thou wouldst have us to believe—that all things are governed by thee, and that nothing takes place except through thy will, so that in the greatest confusions we may always clearly see thy hand, and that thy counsel is altogether right, and perfectly and singularly wise and just; and may we ever call upon thee and flee to this port—that we are tossed here and there in order that thou mayest nevertheless always sustain us by thine hand until we shall at length be received into that blessed rest which has been procured for us by the blood of thine only-begotten Son. Amen.

43

Brotherly Kindness

Thus speaketh the LORD of hosts, saying, 'Execute true judgment, and shew mercy and compassions every man to his brother.'
—Zechariah 7:9.

The people were so devoted to their ceremonies as to think that the whole of religion consisted in fasting and in similar exercises. And as we are by nature prone to this evil, we ought carefully to consider what the prophet has taught us—that fasting is not simply, or by itself, approved by God, but on account of the end designed by it. Having already shown to the Jews their error in thinking that God could be pacified by ceremonies, he now reminds them of what God mainly requires in his law—that men should observe what is just and right toward one another. It is indeed true that the first part of the law refers to the service due to God, but it is a way which God has commonly adopted, to test the life of men by the duties of the second table, and to show what this part of the law especially requires. Therefore God in this passage, as in many others, does not commend righteous-ness toward men so as to depreciate godliness; for as this far excels everything in the whole world, so we know that in rightly forming the life the beginning ought ever to be made by serving God aright. But as the prophet had to do with hypocrites, he shows that they only trifled with God, while they made much of external things, and at the same time neglected uprightness and the duties of love.

Prayer

Grant, Almighty God, that as thou hast adopted us for this end, that we may show brotherly kindness one toward another and labor for our mutual benefit,—O grant, that we may prove by the whole tenor of our life that we have not been called in vain by thee, but that we may live so in harmony with each other that integrity and innocence may prevail among us; and may we so strive to benefit one another, that thy name may be thus glorified by us, until having at length finished our course, we reach the goal which thou hast set before us, that having at last gone through all the evils of this life, we may come to that blessed rest which has been prepared for us in heaven by Christ our Lord. Amen.

44

Deliverance by Covenant

As for thee also, by the blood of thy covenant I have sent forth thy prisoners out of the pit wherein is no water.—Zechariah 9:11.

He addresses Jerusalem as though he had said, "There is no reason for thee to torment thyself with perplexed and anxious thoughts, for I will accomplish what I have promised—that I would become a deliverer to my people." For this doubt might have occurred to them, "Why does he exhort us to rejoice while the Church of God is still in part captive, and while those who have returned to their country are miserably and cruelly harassed by their enemies?" To this objection Zechariah answers, in the person of God, that God would be able to deliver them, though they were sunk in the deepest gulf. The relation, we know, between God and his people as to the covenant is mutual; it is God's covenant, because it flows from him; it is the covenant of the Church, because it is made for its sake, and laid up, as it were, in its bosom. Now, since God receives you into favor, that ye may be safe, he will therefore deliver the captives of his Church. In short, he means, first, that the Jews were sunk in the deep; and, secondly, that thirst would consume them, so that death was nigh at hand unless they were miraculously delivered by God; but he reminds them that no impediment would prevent God from raising them to light from the deepest darkness.

Prayer

Grant, Almighty God, that as we do not at this day look for a Redeemer to deliver us from temporal miseries, but only carry on a warfare under the banner of the cross until he appear to us from heaven to gather us into his blessed kingdom,—O grant that we may patiently bear all evils and all troubles, and as Christ once for all poured forth the blood of the new and eternal covenant, and gave us also a symbol of it in the Holy Supper, may we, confiding in so sacred a seal, never doubt that he will always be propitious to us, and render manifest to us the fruit of this reconciliation, when, after having supported us for a season under the burden of those miseries by which we are now oppressed, thou gatherest us into that blessed and perfect glory which has been procured for us by the blood of Christ our Lord, and which is daily set before us in his gospel, and laid up for us in heaven, until we at length shall enjoy it through Christ, our only Lord. Amen.

45

An Abundant Blessing

For how great is his goodness, and how great is his beauty! Corn shall make the young men cheerful, and new wine the maids.
—Zechariah 9:17.

The prophet here exclaims at the incredible kindness of God, that the Jews might learn to raise up their thoughts above the world, as though his words were, "No one ought to judge God's favor, of which I have spoken, according to his own doings or conduct or experience; but on the contrary, every one of you ought to be filled with amazement at God's incredible kindness and at his incredible beauty." But by the last word he understands the brightness or splendor which appears in all God's favors and gifts. He then concludes by saying, that the abundance of corn and wine would be so great that young men and young women would eat and drink together, and be fully satisfied. But he speaks not here of God's blessing as though it were an incentive to luxury; but what he means is, that the abundance of provisions would be so great as to be fully sufficient not only for the old, but also for young men and young women.

Prayer

Grant, Almighty God, that as we cannot look for temporal or eternal happiness, except through Christ alone, and as thou settest him forth to us as the only true fountain of all blessings,—O grant that we, being content with the favor offered to us through him, may learn to renounce the whole world, and so strive against all unbelief, that we may not doubt that thou wilt ever be our kind and gracious Father, and fully supply whatever is necessary for our support; and may we at the same time live soberly and temperately so that we may not be under the power of earthly things, but with our hearts raised above, aspire after that heavenly bliss to which thou invitest us, and to which thou also guidest us by such helps as are earthly, so that being really united to our Head we may at length reach that glory which has been procured for us by his own blood. Amen.

46
Promise of Restoration

And I will strengthen the house of Judah, and I will save the house of Joseph, and I will bring them again to place them; for I have mercy upon them: and they shall be as though I had not cast them off: for I *am* the LORD their God, and will hear them.
—Zechariah 10:6.

The work of redemption, the beginning of which the Jews saw, would not be incomplete, for the Lord would at length fulfill what he had begun. And this truth is very useful to us, for we are wont to confine God's promises to a short duration of time, and when we thus include him within our narrow limits, we prevent him from performing what we desire. Therefore, let the example of the return of the people of Israel ever come to our minds, for the Lord had promised by his prophets that they would become very eminent, and in every way rich and happy; but when this did not take place after their return to their country, many of the Jews thought that they had been deceived, as they had expected God to fulfill his word immediately; but they ought to have suspended their hope and expectation until Christ came into the world. The state of the people would be happier than it had been since the ten tribes separated from the kingdom of Judah or from the house of David, for God would gather for himself a Church from all the children of Abraham. Though God had dealt severely with that people, yet his vengeance would not be forever, for he would give place to mercy.

Prayer

Grant, Almighty God, that as we are constrained
continually to groan under the burden of our sins, and
the captivity in which we are held until now justly
exposes us to continual trembling and sorrow,—O
grant that the deliverance already begun may inspire
us with a good hope, so as to expect more from thee
than what we can see with our eyes; and may we
continually call on thee until thou completest what
thou hast begun, and puttest to flight both Satan and
our sins, so that, being in true and full liberty devoted
to thee, we may be partakers of that power which has
already appeared in our Head, until, having at length
passed through all our contests, we may reach that
blessed rest where we shall enjoy the fruit of our
victory in Christ alone our Lord. Amen.

47
Beauty and Bands

And I will feed the flock of slaughter, *even* you, O poor of the flock. And I took unto me two staves; the one I called Beauty, and the other I called Bands; and I fed the flock.—Zechariah 11:7.

God here intimates that he had manifested his care for the whole people, for he had hoped that there were a few sheep yet remaining who were worthy to obtain mercy. As then, some poor sheep might have been found among the impure flock, he did not deem it grievous or burdensome to undertake the office of shepherd in ruling the people. The prophet then says, that he had taken two rods, that he might devote himself in a manner not common to the office of a shepherd. Shepherds were satisfied with one crook; for by rods he means here the crook used by shepherds. As then, every shepherd carried his own crook, the prophet says here that he was furnished with two crooks, or shepherd's staffs, because the Lord surpassed all men in his solicitude in the office of ruling his people. Nothing could have been more perfect in beauty than the government which God had exercised over the Israelites; and hence he compares here his shepherd's staff to beauty, as though he had said, "The order of things was so arranged that nothing better could be imagined." He then mentions unity or concord; and it was the highest favor that God gathered again the scattered Israelites so as to make them one body.

Prayer

Grant, Almighty God, that as thou hast hitherto so kindly showed thyself to be our shepherd, and even our Father, and hast carefully provided for our safety,—O grant that we may not, by our ingratitude, deprive ourselves of thy favors, so as to provoke thine extreme vengeance; but, on the contrary, suffer ourselves to be gently ruled by thee, and render thee due obedience; and as thine only-begotten Son has been set over us by thee as our only true Shepherd, may we hear his voice and willingly obey him, so that we may be able to triumph with thy prophet, that thy staff is sufficient for us, so as to enable us to walk without fear through the valley of the shadow of death, until we shall at length reach that blessed and eternal rest which has been obtained for us by the blood of thine only Son. Amen.

48

True Repentance

And I will pour upon the house of David, and upon the inhabitants of Jerusalem, the spirit of grace and of supplications: and they shall look upon me whom they have pierced, and they shall mourn for him, as one mourneth for *his* only *son*, and shall be in bitterness for him, as one that is in bitterness for *his* firstborn.—Zechariah 12:10.

We see here that not only an external grace or favor was promised to the Jews, but an internal light of faith, the author of which is the Spirit. The words, "They shall look upon me whom they have pierced," are to be taken metaphorically, for the prophet expresses here that the Jews would some time return to a sound mind. For it is a true conversion when men seriously acknowledge that they are at war with God, and that he is their enemy until they are reconciled; for except a sinner sets himself in a manner before God's tribunal, he is never touched by a true feeling of repentance. John says that this prophecy was fulfilled in Christ when his side was pierced by a spear (John 19:37). It was necessary that the visible symbol should be exhibited in the person of Christ, in order that the Jews might know that he was the God who had spoken by the prophets. The Jews then had crucified their God when they grieved his Spirit, but Christ was also as to his flesh pierced by them. Zechariah promises the spirit of repentance to the Jews, and mentions a particular kind of repentance. The beginning of repentance we know is grief.

Prayer

Grant, Almighty God, that since thou hast been pleased to adopt us as thy people, and from being thine enemies, profane and reprobate, to make us the children of Abraham that we might be unto thee a holy heritage,—O grant, that through the whole course of our life we may so repent as to attain unto thy mercy, which is daily set before us in the gospel, and of which thou hast given us a sure pledge in the death of thine only Son, so that we may become more and more humble before thee, and labor to form our life according to the rule of thy righteousness, and so loathe ourselves, that we may at the same time be allured by the sweetness of thy goodness to call upon thee, and that being thus united to thee, we may be more and more confirmed in the faith, until at length we shall reach that blessed rest which has been procured for us by the blood of Christ, thine only Son. Amen.

49
Impure Worship Banished

'And it shall come to pass in that day,' saith the LORD of hosts, *'that I will cut off the names of the idols out of the land, and they shall no more be remembered: and also I will cause the prophets and the unclean spirit to pass out of the land.'*—Zechariah 13:2.

God cannot be rightly worshiped, except all corruptions, inconsistent with his sincere and pure worship, be taken away. But we must at the same time observe, that this effect is ascribed to God's word; for it is that which can drive away and banish all the abominations of falsehood, and whatever is uncongenial to true religion. As then, by the rising of the sun darkness is put to flight, and all things appear distinctly to the view, so also when God comes forth with the teaching of his word, all the deceptions of Satan must necessarily be dissipated. Whosoever then, desires to perform all the duties of a good and faithful pastor, ought firmly to resolve, not only to abstain from all impure doctrines and simply to assert what is true, but also to detect all corruptions which are injurious to religion, to recover men from the deceptions of Satan, and in short, avowedly to carry on war with all superstitions. We may learn how much purity of doctrine is approved by God, since he would have us feel a horror as at something monstrous, whenever the name of an idol is mentioned. The Church cannot be preserved in a pure state except the rashness of those who pervert sound doctrine be restrained.

Prayer

Grant, Almighty God, that as thou hast been pleased to draw us at this day by the light of thy gospel, out of that horrible darkness in which we have been miserably immersed, and to render thy face so conspicuous to us in the person of thine only-begotten Son, that nothing but our ingratitude prevents us from being transformed into thy celestial glory,—O grant that we may make such advances in the light of truth, that every one of us may be ashamed of his former ignorance, and that we may freely and ingenuously confess that we were lost sheep, until we were brought back into the way of salvation by thy hand; and may we thus proceed in the course of our holy calling until we shall at length be all gathered into heaven, where not only that truth shall give us light, which now rules us according to the capacity of our flesh, but where also the splendor of thy glory shall shine in us, and shall render us conformable to thine image, through Christ alone our Lord. Amen.

50

Saved by Grace

'I have loved you,' saith the LORD. Yet ye say, 'Wherein hast thou loved us?' '*Was* not Esau Jacob's brother?' saith the LORD: 'yet I loved Jacob'.—Malachi 1:2.

When God says that he loved the Jews, his object was to convict them of ingratitude for having despised the singular favor bestowed on them alone, rather than to press that authority which he possesses over all mankind in common. The origin of all the excellency which belonged to the posterity of Abraham is here ascribed to the gratuitous love of God, according to what Moses often said, "Not because ye excelled other nations, or were more in number, has God honored you with so many benefits, but because he loved your fathers." We see that we differ from animals because God was pleased to create us men. He therefore will justly charge us with ingratitude if we do not serve him, for it was for this end he created us in his own image. But there is here mentioned a special favor— that the Lord took to himself the seed of Abraham, as it is said in the song of Moses, that all nations are God's, but that he had cast his line to set apart Israel for himself (Deut. 32:9). By love he means gratuitous favor. There is no reason for us to seek any other cause for adoption except the will of God. God's free favor and gratuitous mercy prevails as to individuals.

Prayer

Grant, Almighty God, that as thou hast been pleased to adopt us once for all as thy people for this end, that we may be engrafted, as it were, into the body of thy Son, and so be made conformable to our Head,—O grant that through our whole life we may strive to seal in our hearts the faith of our election, that we may be the more stimulated to render thee true obedience, and that thy glory may also be made known through us; and those others also whom thou hast chosen together with us may we labor to bring with us, that we may with one accord celebrate thee as the Author of our salvation, and so ascribe to thee the glory of thy goodness, that having cast away and renounced all confidence in our own virtue, we may be led to Christ only as the fountain of thy election, in whom also is set before us the certainty of our salvation through thy gospel, until we shall at length be gathered with him into that eternal glory which he has procured for us by his own blood. Amen.

51
The Calling of the Gentiles

For from the rising of the sun even unto the going down of the same my name *shall be* great among the Gentiles; and in every place incense *shall be* offered unto my name, and a pure offering: for my name *shall be* great among the heathen, saith the LORD of hosts.
—Malachi 1:11.

The prophets promised to the Jews that the Gentiles would become allied to them; so does Zechariah, "In those days it shall come to pass, that ten men shall take hold . . . of the skirt of him that is a Jew, saying, 'We will go with you: for we have heard that God is with you'" (Zech. 8:23). It would have been then the highest honor to the Jews had they become teachers to all nations, so as to instruct them in the true religion. So also Isaiah says that those who were before aliens would become the disciples of the chosen people, so that they would willingly submit to their teaching. But as the Jews have fallen from their place, the Gentiles have succeeded and occupied their position; according to what Christ threatened to men of his age, "The kingdom of God shall be taken from you and given to a nation bringing forth the fruits thereof" (Matthew 21:43). The calling of the Gentiles is here clearly proved, because the name of God cannot be great without the teaching of the truth. It is therefore the same thing as though the prophet had said that the law which had been given to the Jews would be proclaimed among all nations.

Prayer

Grant, Almighty God, that since thou dost not keep us at this day under the shadows of the law, by which thou didst train up the race of Abraham, but invitest us to a service far more excellent, even to consecrate ourselves body and soul as victims to thee, and to offer not only ourselves, but also sacrifices of praise and of prayer, as thou hast consecrated all the duties of religion which thou requirest from us through Christ thy Son,—O grant, that we may seek true purity and labor to render our services approved by thee by a real sincerity of heart, and so reverently profess and call upon thy name that it may be truly acknowledged as fulfilled in us, which thou hast declared by thy prophet—that undoubtedly thy name shall be magnified and celebrated throughout the whole world, as it was truly made known to us in the very person of thine only-begotten Son. Amen.

52
Christ's Forerunner

Behold, I will send you Elijah the prophet before the coming of the great and dreadful day of the LORD.—Malachi 4:5.

The prophet having testified to the Jews, that though God would for a time suspend the course of prophetic teaching, they yet had in the law what was sufficient for salvation, he now promises the renovation of the Church, as though he had said, "The Lord will again unexpectedly utter his voice after a long silence." Isaiah speaks on the same subject prophesying of the return of the people when he says, "Comfort ye, comfort ye my people, will our God say" (Isaiah 40:1). At the same time he shows that the time would come, when his purpose was to confirm and seal all the prophesies by his only-begotten Son. Christ himself said that John the Baptist was the Elijah who had been promised (Matthew 11:14). God intended to raise up John the Baptist for the purpose of restoring his worship, as formerly he had raised up Elijah, for at the time of Elijah, we know, that not only the truth was corrupted, and the worship of God vitiated, but also that all religion was well-nigh extinct, so that nothing pure and sound remained. At the coming of Christ, though the Jews did not worship idols, but retained some outward form of religion, yet the whole of their religion was spurious, so that that time may truly be compared, on account of its multiplied pollutions, to the age of Elijah.

Prayer

Grant, Almighty God, that as nothing has been omitted by thee to help us onward in the course of our faith, and as our sloth is such that we hardly advance one step though stimulated by thee,—O grant that we may strive to profit more by the various helps which thou hast provided for us, so that the law, the prophets, the voice of John the Baptist, and especially the doctrine of thine only-begotten Son, may more fully awaken us, that we may not only hasten to him, but also proceed constantly in this course, and persevere in it until we shall at length obtain both the victory and the crown of our calling, as thou hast promised an eternal inheritance reserved in heaven for all who faint not, but wait for the coming of that great Redeemer. Amen.

Other SGCB Classic Reprints

Solid Ground Christian Books is honored to present the following titles, many for the first time in more than a century:

Call us Toll Free at 1-877-666-9469
Send us an e-mail at sgcb@charter.net
Visit us on line at solid-ground-books.com

Uncovering Buried Treasure to the Glory of God

Printed in the United Kingdom
by Lightning Source UK Ltd.
103786UKS00001B/73-93